Wear
Sunscreen

**Andrews McMeel
Publishing**

Kansas City

Wear Sunscreen

A Primer for Real Life

MARY SCHMICH

To my mother,

who was wise enough

not to burden

her eight children

with advice.

~~~~~~~~~~~~~

www.andrewsmcmeel.com

ISBN: 0-8362-5528-3

Library of Congress: 97-80367

Design by: Mauna Eichner

ACKNOWLEDGMENTS

All the people who are important to me—friends, relations, muses—are lurking in the lines of this book. I won't name them, but without their inspiration over the years, I never would have written this column, perhaps would never have written anything at all. I owe a special thank-you to Dave Burgin, my first editor and a newspaperman like no other, who gave me the courage of my voice.

INTRODUCTION

Most of us live life in a haze of days. One day we eat, we drink, we work, we shop, we sleep, we brush our teeth. The next day we do it all again. Occasionally in the blur of routine tasks, we have a clear thought about how we live and how we'd like to, and notice with distress that the two are not the same.

These were the kinds of lofty thoughts I was thinking one day in May as I walked along Lake Michigan to my job at the *Chicago Tribune*. I write a column for the paper three times a week and, on that morning, with another column deadline barreling toward me, I had loads of thoughts on life but not a single thought for a column.

Then I saw her, a woman in her twenties sitting on the lakefront, her face turned toward the sun to catch the weak May rays. "I hope that woman's wearing sunscreen," I clucked to myself.

I realized in that moment that I'd reached a dangerous phase of life, the phase in which a person is seized by the desire to redeem her own mistakes by administering advice. I also realized it was graduation time, a time when speakers everywhere could sow their words of wisdom without seeming like buffoons.

Okay, so no one had invited me to be a graduation speaker. Why not pretend?

I spent the afternoon, fueled by coffee and M&M's, composing the graduation speech I would give if anyone bothered to ask. I encouraged readers to try writing their own speech, mostly as a way to discover, as I did in the process, how they would sum up the lessons of their life.

The column ran in the paper on Sunday, June 1, 1997. And that was that.

Until two months later.

On a Friday in August, I learned that some unknown person at some unknown time for some unknown reason had stripped my name off my mock graduation speech—which was posted on the *Tribune*'s web site—and sent it into cyber-space. Out in the vast, ungoverned cyberfrontier, a different, legendary name was attached: Kurt Vonnegut.

Before long, my simple little column was rocketing around the world on the Internet, from England to Australia, from Costa Rica to Japan to New Zealand, disguised as a famous 75-year-old author's graduation speech to the Massachusetts Institute of Technology. When word of the mistaken identity of the "sunscreen" speech finally became public, the mix-up became national news, widely publicized evidence of yet another example of the power and the perils of the Internet. Despite all the publicity, no one ever figured out how or why I became Kurt Vonnegut.

Whatever the source of this odd cybersnafu, I continue to be amazed and grateful that so many people from so many places have appreciated these few words. Even now, people around the world send me e-mail saying they've just received the speech, or just learned its true origin. Some ask if I have more advice.

I don't. Except for this:

Do your work. You never know when routine life will delight and surprise you.

Ladies and
Gentlemen,

Wear sunscreen.

If I could offer you only
        one tip for the future,
    sunscreen would be it.

The long-term benefits of
   sunscreen have been proved
      by scientists, whereas the rest
of my advice has no basis more
reliable than my own
            meandering experience.

I will dispense this advice now.

Enjoy the power and

beauty of your youth.

Oh, never mind.

You will not understand
the power and beauty
of your youth until
they've faded.

But trust me,

    in twenty years, you'll look back
at photos of yourself and recall

    in a way you can't grasp now
how much possibility lay before you

    and how fabulous you really looked.

You are not as fat as you imagine.

Don't worry about the future.
Or worry,
but know that worrying is as
effective as trying to
solve an algebra equation
by chewing bubble gum.

The real troubles in your life
are apt to be things
that never crossed
your worried mind,
the kind that blindside you at
four P.M. on some idle Tuesday.

Do
one
thing
every
day
that
scares
you.

Sing.

Don't be reckless
with
other people's hearts.

Don't put up with people
who are
reckless with yours.

Floss.

Don't waste your time on jealousy.

Sometimes you're ahead,

sometimes you're behind.

The race is long and,
in the end,
it's only with yourself.

Remember
compliments
you receive.

Forget the insults.

If you succeed in doing this,

tell me how.

Keep your old love letters.

Throw away
your old bank statements.

Stre

tch.

Don't feel guilty if you don't
know what you want to do
with your life.
The most interesting people
I know didn't know at twenty-two
what they wanted to do with
their lives.

Some of the most interesting

forty-year-olds I know still don't.

Get plenty of calcium.

Be kind to your knees.
You'll miss them when they're
gone.

Maybe you'll marry,
maybe you won't.

Maybe you'll have children,
maybe you won't.

Maybe you'll divorce at forty,

maybe you'll dance the
funky chicken
on your seventy-fifth
wedding anniversary.

Whatever you do,
    don't congratulate yourself
        too much, or
    berate yourself either.

Your choices are half chance.

So are everybody else's.

Enjoy your body.

Use it

every way

you can.

Don't be afraid of it
or of what other people think
of it.
It's the greatest instrument
you'll ever own.

Dance,

even if

you have

nowhere

to do it

but your

living room.

Read the
directions,
even if
you don't
follow them.

Do not read beauty magazines.

They will only
make you feel ugly.

Get to know your parents.
You never know
when they'll be gone for good.

Be nice to your siblings.
They're your best link to your past
and the people most likely
to stick with you in the future.

Understand that friends
come and go, but with
a precious few
you should hold on.

Work hard to bridge the gaps
in geography and lifestyle,
because the older you get,
the more you need the people
who knew you
when you were young.

Live in
New York City
once,
but leave
before it makes you hard.

Live in
Northern California
once,
but leave
before it makes you soft.

Travel.

Accept certain
inalienable truths:
                    Prices will rise.
Politicians will philander.
          You, too, will get old.

And when you do,
you'll fantasize that when you
were young,
          prices were reasonable,
politicians were noble,
          and children respected
                    their elders.

Respect your elders.

Don't expect anyone else

to support you.

Maybe you have a trust fund.
Maybe you'll have
a wealthy spouse.
But you never know
when either one might
run out.

Don't mess too much

with your hair

or by the time you're forty

it will look eighty-five.

Be careful whose advice you buy,
but be patient
with those who
supply it.

Advice is a form of nostalgia.

Dispensing it is a way of
fishing the past from the disposal,
wiping it off,
painting over the ugly parts, and
recycling it for more than it's worth.

But trust me on the sunscreen.